ONLY AND AGAIN

Dustin Pickering

ONLY AND AGAIN
By
Dustin Pickering

Setu Publications
* Pittsburgh, PA (USA) *
© 2021 by Dustin Pickering

ISBN-13 (paperback): 978-1-947403-13-0
Cover image: Abyss of floating dreams, Sufia Khatoon
All illustrations (c) Sufia Khatoon, 2021

All rights reserved. No part of this work may be reproduced, translated, recorded, stored, transmitted, or displayed in any form, or by any means electronic, mechanical, or otherwise without the prior written permission of the author, the copyright owner except for brief quotations in book reviews, and as otherwise permitted by applicable law. Any such quotations must acknowledge the source.
We would be pleased to receive email correspondence regarding this publication or related topics at setuedit@gmail.com.

Distributed to the book trade worldwide by Setu Publications, Pittsburgh (USA)

Although every precaution has been taken in the preparation of this work, neither the author nor the publisher shall have any liability to any person or entity with respect to any loss or damage caused or alleged to be caused directly or indirectly by the information contained in this work.

Setu Literary Publications, Pittsburgh, USA

ONLY AND AGAIN

*"If we shadows have offended,
Think but this, and all is mended,
That you have but slumber'd here
While these visions did appear.
And this weak and idle theme,
No more yielding but a dream,
Gentles, do not reprehend:
if you pardon, we will mend:
And, as I am an honest Puck,
If we have unearned luck
Now to 'scape the serpent's tongue,
We will make amends ere long;
Else the Puck a liar call;
So, good night unto you all.
Give me your hands, if we be friends,
And Robin shall restore amends."*

A Midsummer Night's Dream

Contents

Artist Note 11
INTRODUCTION 13
DARKLING 17
    i. 17
Venus de Milo 17
Everlasting Kiss 20
Madonna lost to the black 22
shield of memory 23
Oligarchy 28
Walpurgis Night 29
Passion in Primrose 30
Father, Absent 31
Darling 32
One Page Beyond 33
Spinoza's Crust of Bread 34
The Infinitely Tall 36
As Often I Trouble 38
Escape 39
Books Bound by Leather 40
Milk 41
A Mind's Aggression 42
Stubbornly Silent 43
Perpetual Slumber 44
As Coils the Prayer 45
Void 46

Counting Days	47
Casual Acquaintance	48
Repetition	49
QUEEN MABUS	50
Invocation to Muse Anna	51
i. The Surrender	52
ii. Questions for the Damned	57
iii.	61
iv. Carmel Lips	72
Addendum:	78
COUCHED LIKE ROBINSON CRUSOE	79
i. Pastures of Plenty	79
inspiration	92
apex of time	93
gestalt	94
broken stone	95
EPILOGUE	96
The Kristal Palace	96

Artist Note

Any form of art born within a person, travels through him/her, reflects his/her immediate reality and becomes a part of the entire universe. I believe we are mediums to the infinite light guiding, controlling, healing the world around us all. Illustrating Dustin Pickering's book, especially the poems, defines this very belief of mine. We are bubbles of energy passing this infinite light through our art to one another, so we can find comfort in these uncertain times. Be strong and become warmth to one another. Each illustration has a story behind it, passing through hours of restlessness of my mind and finally transforming on the paper. This is the beauty of the forms of art we have been blessed with. I wish this book touches and heals hearts as the years move with time.

Sufia Khatoon.

ONLY AND AGAIN

INTRODUCTION

The Muse as Dynamic Flow

"Every investigation implies the idea of nudity which one brings out into the open by clearing away the obstacles which cover it, just as Actaeon clears away the branches so that he can have a better view of Diana at her bath."

Jean-Paul Sartre, *Being and Nothingness*

Sexuality is a dynamic energy that permeates Being. The Muse is an energy that permeates life with creative flow and compassion. In these poems, I give three muses their due: Lisa Marie Basile, Anna Suarez, and Monica Lewis, all poets in their own right. Their creative capacities are admirable and their physical beauty is as well.

A muse does not appear, but simply is, like consciousness resting within us. She is to be realized, not apprehended, as she is not a victim or criminal. She is the spirit of beauty encapsulating all things, even the hideous and deformed. The Muse is not the observer, but is the transparency of observation. She is Diana and I, the onlooker, am Actaeon. To look is also to be transformed by the privilege of envisioning beauty. "The gaze" is a form of possession—to look upon someone is to apprehend them by transfixing their form in one's own eye. However, the Muse is elusive. She knows the eye and likes to play. She runs through the forests. She is knowledge itself.

Knowledge is self-knowledge at its height. One studies to realize oneself and what one truly values. A reader will shed pretension and the desire to overpower. When knowledge is used to illuminate, it becomes a faith that empowers all it touches. Beauty is a thing without utility. It is superfluous, but it heightens our prowess and joy in life and its spectacle.

I present the reader with three lovely women whose presence embodied the Muse for me at differing points. Because the Muse is otherworldly, she inhabits space but does not present her actual Being to us. Hence, we are unable to have a complete view of her and cannot marry her. This is why we are deformed by comparison. The material world is conventionally masculine—it is strength, power, and boldness. The spiritual world is feminine—it is grace, charm, beauty, and art.

In truth, Actaeon resides outside the universe as we know it—he is the observer. The bathing is the universe making and unmaking itself. Once it imagines itself observed, it becomes ashamed and tries to hide. In its hiding, it evades us perpetually. The world is a dynamic flow of energies. It is constancy which gives it shape and structure.

Diana, moon goddess and chaste woman, is the Madonna of creation. Her dynamic flow is uninterrupted. It is perfect, graceful, and abundant.

Sexuality is the flow of Being from one point to another. It is the energy that binds, ties, unites. It is the essence of being human. Beyond its biological consequences, it is the appreciation of beauty and the feeling of awe that permeates us in wonder.

These poems strive to express this powerful realization. They are divided into eight sections total to represent the phases of the moon.

ONLY AND AGAIN

ONLY AND AGAIN

DARKLING

angels announcing

for Lisa Marie Basile

i.

Venus de Milo

Am I the pearl in your mouth as you speak?
How does love announce its wings?

I steer in the streets like an ancient schizoid,
relentless in battle with the organs of fire.

The magic of sound alights the roaring tempest
of your clear body, singing the trees.

If night will bend to me and my kisses on your ink,
I will make the fists of God into minted elm.

The sea is one nocturnal emphasis:
I speak to you across distances like a code
in war. The mothers of the universe are your whores.
I am your daughter, and you are roses in bloom.
I know this because I was an empty blossom
holding your tongue in eclipse. Science doesn't attempt.
I am a fighter in the flight for fancy
and Lolita limps to my lights. I am drunk on the wine of song:
the ships of ghost wars fight and kiss your lips
with the redness of lustful season.

I know you like the visions of Mary
and the archangels who storm the eyes.
Everything I am is born of your love:
assay, great in ecstasy.

We are Romans in pissing pleasure

ONLY AND AGAIN

while the ancients sell their wares
in the exotic heights...
yet the tracks are unknown
and the Promised Land is made of thunder again.
You can't sing when your nights are lost.

I am not smoking song
and I invite comparison.
Skeleton keys cannot open your secret chambers;
the wounds of destiny are left to fester like moss in clay.

ONLY AND AGAIN

Everlasting Kiss

ONLY AND AGAIN

o and if I love you
the muses will know
but they keep their secrets
in the shadows of the will

I am hiding in a window
looking at the sun opening eyes
imagining the sorcery of your vision

if I were the fingers launching your poem,
lurching as the envoy while you gaze reluctantly at sunbeams
dying on the apocalyptic highway,
a dream or thought would enter me.
everyone glares at the gems
decadently strewn through your hair
because you are the prime beauty
of the everlasting kiss

...and jealousy is a tightly clinched fist

Dustin Pickering

Madonna lost to the black

on Munch's Madonna

What am I to again seek?
The arms of Madonna
bright and pensive
keeping her eyes for the lost
and losing her speech?...
mute as a diamond in the sky
sunk in venomous tar,
thickened by the embryo
of love, of love
the angel in flight

kiss me, dove
and make my engines roar
as only lions know
the colors of your youth

I know these wounded streets
like the laws of my hand
and the lingering sounds of flutes
die finally when you embrace ritual

dove, you are the animal
of haunted auditoriums
the sea is a tyrant clutching your hand
and drowning my mind
against the intensity of your parallels
everything is empty as a seashell
lost to the black

shield of memory

You are my rosary of depth
and I pray the rays of your beads
as the night remembers it's trying losses
mourning is a private sky

I want to hold you like a star as it dies and collapses
ignoring paupers offering street wisdom
dope dealers tell me what they stole
as the marching band celebrates the last kiss

my soul is a city reaching to you like arms in the bedroom
I want to surrender myself to you
words are only the dreams I invent
like twin guns facing the enemy

salt will conserve our victory
I am yours eternally like a shield of memory

ONLY AND AGAIN

look westward as a child
face the mother of our burning surrender
with one another we dance the empty flesh
that spirit becomes

I haven't imprisoned the intensity of my passion,
not yet but moments come and go

the rain echoes across your immaculate light like a prison
but only I can reveal your freedom and crime
theft of broken hearts and roses grown of death and sagacity
everything is torn from me like a bone whispering in dirt

if the flutes of fortune imply magical faith
I embrace fiat in the wake of swollen bellies
and hearts, every face of your prime

depth is the soul of our war
I can only love you as an urchin of fashion
don't gaze inward or the starlings will tell secrets

ONLY AND AGAIN

I can't collide
we won't know one another
until our dimensions reveal each other
to questioning ghosts—
the darkness knows what we will become

every light was once a snake of senses
but you are the most gracious of beings
holding the flame like a maiden
prepared for the mischief of sex and grace

we are brazed torches lit for beauty
we are universal
the hideousness of plight is war to the wise

ONLY AND AGAIN

I am sick with your delight
wine to the eyes
of your magic
like a continuous crime against my ugly shame

you make me rise to the patriotic alarum
and tell it to fuck off
as the last of tycoons dies in perverse loneliness

drive me mad you
treasure and witch of mad mind
plotting the windows of my efforts
you are secretly exact—
nothing you do is mistake
desperation is night cold and bright

I only see what I am inclined to know
you are like a sprite of arched premise
we all know where the story leads

the lion is tied in private corridors of flesh
his eyes are bright coals of thought
breathing from the brainstem to lit areas
of the imagination

only I can love the fantasy I created

I love you as only a stranger could
distance is magic to spirits of attraction
you are my life, my wound, my darkling
and I can only thank you for such liberation….

ii.

ONLY AND AGAIN

Tinfoil.
The moon taken,
colliding with eyes fill'd
tempestuously with grief.

You are overtaken
by the memories
and filled with star's wonder
at the harmony flitting in your veins.

I can't ask questions
when your bearing is silent.
Someone should hold you quietly
and tell you Love is listening.

Oligarchy

The wealthy hold the wares
but they have not seen your lips
part in thoughtless frivolity;
not the way I have in the least.

Walpurgis Night

Sink deeper into the dark crater
where hobgoblins fester in horror—
Walpurgis night.

Everything I am sees you in a different light.
Perhaps you aren't used to the sad eagles
of reclusive thought.
Did someone ask you to make things difficult?

Imagine for a second your face painted by da Vinci.
With his charm and complacency intact.
You then momentarily arc
into a goddess of the full moon.

The owls are glaring—
and the wolves are bending their knees
on the forest floor.

Passion in Primrose

Tiny flower, held with seriousness
and imagination,
you are unaffected by the world we know.
You are outside of human trappings.

I make a tiny necklace from little yellow flowers.
I bestow them on you...
you smile like a snail in glee.
Your eyes dance like lightning at a funeral.

I won't suffer now.
I am blind in the season of forgetting.
Your carriage will bring you as far as *here*—
it won't take you further.

Father, Absent

The jar holds many coins.
I look at it as at any other object.
Its meaninglessness doesn't arouse me.

My father walks in, graceful as a shadow,
and mutters incoherent profanity to himself.
He lifts the jar up, speaks—
"Son, this is your future. Don't let go of it."

I couldn't hear his words.

Darling

If existence is having only enough
tunnel vision to know hope—
let me exist but also let me plead.
I do not know much else.

The light at the end?
It is a racketeering scheme.
The darkness I am encased within?
The truth, it will set you free.

I have grown so tall that my head
hits the top of the tunnel,
often painfully.
I've killed my darlings.

One Page Beyond

I am not known for patience.
I don't consider it a virtue.
Why wait when there is no need?

When I read beautiful words,
unfathomable,
it is like being swallowed by a whale.

I open the book and seek its poetry.
I turn page after page,
skipping the less attractive words.

The whale spits me out
and my hair is full of kelp.
I am pleasantly silent.

ONLY AND AGAIN

Spinoza's Crust of Bread

Traitorous angel,
fix fast on sighs
that create mountains and sift
the trees,
delicately flirting with their branches.

Spinoza sits in a quiet room,
so dark he cannot see his eyes.
His eyes are all that exist.
A window is open but only the night
speaks through it.
Nothing but shapeless vanity.

He dips his crust in milk,
wondering if the act is symbolic
of the Old Soul within us all.
He is the demiurge and Madonna
of Nature,

thickening by pulse
what is lost in fame.

ONLY AND AGAIN

The Infinitely Tall

ONLY AND AGAIN

As hummingbird with devil's eye,
I bat my wings until I reach the height
I envision with my sound lights.

Libraries, like trees, have rings
that measure age.
Shelves are like ladder rungs.

A bookcase holding tomes of ideas
arranged in synthesis,
a timeless constant.

I immediately reach a point of pause.
I am an arm's distance from the shelves.
Perhaps reaching, I will catch the mystery.

Like eggs in the nest
the books rest against time,
immemorial in thriftiness.

The bookcase reaches high,
unfathomably high...
I travel as skyward as I desire.

As Often I Trouble

As often I trouble the Muses
for their elixir,
they should retire into the clouds
and refuse to serve me.

It's like being at a bar
and constantly flirting with the waitress.
I never buy anything,
but talk about everything.

Hocus Pocus—
a night on the silence
like a rock 'n' roll highway.
Even deafening noise embalms.

iii.

Escape

The crystal road is translucent,
ducked in splendor and bright ecstasy.

I carry the dreams of rotten whores
on my back, tedium reaching its summit.

The blades of my back stiffen
and edge out their mountains.

I am my own holiness, sharp
and cringing at the delight of names.

Words describe my plush tomes.
I don't know where to find my home.

I traverse this road, tired and patient.
I won't find God. I won't rejoice.

Books Bound by Leather

These words and their sores
are bound in thick leather,
soft and lustful to the eyes.

A man signals a caravan
in Greek symbols.

We know our past by the lives
it shattered.
We don't know the night is long.

Dark, not dismal, are interior monologues.
Words burn through the skull.
Ripe, plucking the skin from its house,
a sentence strains within the cranium.
It finds nothing to cling to.

Its victims are strapped to silence,
all-envisioning
yet knowing virtually nothing.

Milk

Milk thick and white as teeth,

open mouth,
                    coursing through the silence...
addressing tongues of fire
and birthing baptisms.

Only the lurch of forgiveness
woven within the architecture of light

all else is empty

all is dream

the clouds are wisps of wandering
as veils forked with lightning—
find the source
                  and look underneath

A Mind's Aggression

Does the minotaur know
I find knots in the yarn

                    that led me here
and will lift them
from the floor of the maze?

Stubbornly Silent

When I release joy—
        it is something to release,
the world grows deeper by its pause—
flowers bloom in soft stillness
                like echoes of origins,
the immediate answer to thoughts.

To suffer motion
                        and bear each witness as gifts
from the horizon of eyes—
                            Glory is genuine,
thought betrays—

Night opens to rays released while my tongue staggers in the wayside of thought,
        but what if I am dream?

Perpetual Slumber

I fall into stars as a noose falls against the neck it hangs
My death thickens like blood hammered to the wind

Everything—even frozen suffrage—will weaken, fall
as the time's crushing ballad becomes purple,
                    reigning as Paradise in a fickle heart.

Eat the crumbs of bread that drop near your feet.
Fall to victim as a short humility. I sing a sordid fallacy—
                night dreams and desires,
but wait: nothing is there.
The banquet is a mob of pleasure seeking soldiers—
                hedonists of wind,
Epicurus's flight of fancy into emptiness
                where refuge is deep silence.

As Coils the Prayer

As coils the prayer, a balm of imagination
                is proven
           through vision's entry into power.
A forsaken tempest of fight-or-flight fancy.

Open and entertain the theater of consequence.
A marriage of delight will be a last forgetting.
              Look where the water falls
      from a broken edge,
           cliffs where pleasant sun
                  balances in the stolen effigies of creeping vine...

The magic foments in delirium,
              again I am sad,
but enter the force of intuition:
treat the memories as blood staining the mirror of your being.

Void

All is relentless—
the earth flows with rancid blood,
        a lost open dream where magnitude
        hides like a riot in a broken body.

Gems stolen from your eyes,
        replace them with hideous allure
cosmic brokenness—
ancient flowers dry on the path.
        I look for water,
search in the godless hours
for a lustful taste,
        something less concrete than a windowsill.

If a globe wants shadow,
some lust—bright, beaming, sky of emptiness...

I am perplexed—
nothing is our radiance.
We simply are.

Counting Days

When light
        left her eyes,
        darkness turned to stone.
In grace, we ponder
        the forgotten.
3,000 minutes strive to build minuets
  of perplexed domain—
a struggle in fiery forests of friendship.

Hosts know their prey:
it is unforgettable,
        the sweetness of Being.

How do we count the days?
Are there thoughts hidden in short crevices
        of lost energies?
How do we know?

Nigh we will seek high fields of grace—
an atomic permissiveness,
        all we know, universe.

Casual Acquaintance

They robbed
        in robes covered in glee
There were stiff fists of cliché
          hording over the isolated night

Once distress entered our hearts—
      we knew, oh, we knew

Shame of my rightful love.
I felt the climb forward. And I was shy.

After all,
we didn't know each other—
only faces of black doubt entered as dormant guests.
An instinct.

        I was wearing muddied pants, a strange guest—
the most righteous know the glare of truth.

I will be the fool
and I will dream
somehow guessing at last days.

Repetition

Birth will stain me
and I will remember
the silence of night

        A star is a word,
        bees' wanderlust and grateful image

A fast thought
        cannot be contained—
let me loosen the hybrid autonomy of humanity.

Moon:granted you will know. Fall.
Let me stick knives into your eyes—
        as night engages a topless dancer
        in dark remiss.
My silence is a letter,

                                                                              bombed

to no avail
        like longing in the shadows.

Whose word against mine?
Again.
Say the final word.
Again.
Again.

QUEEN MABUS

"Light of my life, fire of my loins, be a good baby, do what I want..."
Lana del Rey, "Off to the Races"

dedicated to Anna Suarez, poet of "Papi Doesn't Love Me Anymore"

Invocation to Muse Anna

Open mouths don't tell the secrets they wish to tell.
Instead, they dream the anchor that yields to the river.
The sea does not contemplate; it only hears. And it whispers.

But in your yearning you do not see me yearning.
The dawn is one giant viper spitting its frenzy
like a cold dew flying from an old regime flag
as it shakes to the ground.

O! the night is somber and your eyes make me wonder
what this gift of life means. Truly, I speak to you in this wonder.

ONLY AND AGAIN

i. The Surrender

The time was perilous for me. I yearned to be completely free
yet I was chained to poisonous rapture.
This rapture was my will to beat my vans against the cold night air,
empty and joyous. The laughter of the crows, a crowd of ancient lips.

They ached to hear the sounds. My ears lean to the ground.
I hear all the dead earth. Your face beams like a ray from a prism
into the winter. But I see nothing in you but dread,
and my touch will not satisfy your yearning. But you said.

If silence is what you crave (and I doubt it is silence as much as a space
to call your own), my mind will give it to you. The eyes I rip from my
face
only know their mother from the kind shelter of light.
Mothers don't weep but they err, and they err hard and deep.
They cannot step the hurdles twice; this knife is my eye.

I grab fast the masked race of dawn. But knowledge is my epigenetic
crucible.
You were staring at me, in this winter, but I did not think twice to
remind you.

ONLY AND AGAIN

I let the surrender come to me. The violence of poison
stuck in my skull as only a dusky aurora.
Your eyes catch me in hiding but I was in pure oblivion—
from which you rescue my fallenness.

If I am insane, I will hold the hand of everything
until my boredom splits to tears
because love is this shadow of mirth I cannot complete.
Being impure, I only know the body from its sound—

your eyes catch me in the fathomless dark
where I don't understand anything.

They medicate me and entice me from the womb
because insanity is like being born again,
knowing the topical aroma of death.
However my scream to touch you will only seek the breast,
biting back as a babe, knowing want, thinking heavy on my own winter.

Dustin Pickering

ONLY AND AGAIN

I want to offer you something. Understanding.
I hope you will not fear me.
Because I am lost to the dozen of small roses

I granted you as a first sense. You weren't alive yet,
but we knew the magic of bliss. Rapture torn from the eyes.

Vision is tunneling your ecstasy from whatever cold night you slumber—
slumber only being a metaphor for the people you met waking.

If your eyes were plum and fairy, I could not touch you with this imagination.
Spring alights the fury of life like a chariot flowering the highway with fire.

ONLY AND AGAIN

These wonders only the sky knows—
thoughts arranging like lilies on the water
in a spring of perfect contentment.

The water is a mirror to your mind,
sensuous and starving—
the night frozen against your eyes
as a starlet in flustered drama.

Your mind is a door to the open womb.
Your mind is a flesh in its own harrowing.
O light, do not starve this baby's eyes.

We are together. My mind and myself.
We hold hands on the open road.
The road so delightful that flowers spill
onto it from the kissing of lovers.

And I know your phantoms from the bliss they harangue.
There is nothing here but darkness and a sky.

ONLY AND AGAIN

If the rise is unleavened,
do you know the whispers from their abandon?
How do we kiss in darkness perplexed by imagination?

Is fantasy a warrior for the dreams we cherish
or do we hide from the Actual by palming the sweetness?

What vapid trust secures the antagonism that created us?
Were we born of fury and blood?
Does trust impale us as only fears of our heart?
What then, of this satisfaction I feel in gazing
into you and watching your eyes palliate the lost?

ii. Questions for the Damned

Do devils pick your eyes with a fine toothed comb?
Do they incite rapture? Is ecstasy the triumph of your fear
over love and denial?
What about the children you claim to adore?

o Madonna of the silence, do you make the hours weep?

But what is this hiddenness? how can we sense the gloom
between midnight and the listless hours?
I can hear them screaming. I can hear them wanting to come alive,
again, like tears from the eyes of willows.

But if you strain long enough to hear the deep flask
of solitude, rewards will be plenty:
your damnation will be rewarding.

ONLY AND AGAIN

As you stand, dancing among the primrose,
thinking of guardians who pose the Word:
your corridors are flaming with song,
and your master calls from behind the masque.

But you only know terror and blood,
the reign of sorcery:
the last rite of timelessness.

And I hate the eyes you carry like a torch,
thinking of the books I wrote to you,
wishing for a time you were alive.

Yet I know you aren't what I claimed you were.
In the night you became something in excelsior—
a goddess of tombs, thoughtless yet savvy.

And the ancients heard. They knew what you were singing.

ONLY AND AGAIN

Wipe the sullen speech from those lips.
You do not know despair. You only think on it.
The poem will tell you.

Bottom's dream is paradise if eternity was cyclical
like your passion and imagination—
o rose of youth, tumble to this living flight.

I do not stand behind you in the lost abeyance
of fruit. This is what they call your energy.
Your thrust like a sword through my eyes.

I dream of your tall tales and fairy queen nonchalance.
Do you care to kill me with a thought?
Do secrets break open like seeds?
What do you see in the deadend night?

Are lights really the sparkles of your faith?

ONLY AND AGAIN

Byzantine thoughts pass the empire.
Your tigerlily vision is wanton with worship.
Yet I do not know how much light
can pour into your vessels.

If I open the doorway to your longing,
please kiss me deeply like a river
of lust: speak, ocean, to this tyranny.
The death of millions is upon you.

Her moon soft glow reaches the fertility
of her mind. She becomes an age of Being.
The coldness between her lips
is only a hidden sacrifice.

We as traitors only know the worrisome.
Love will guide you
in this fearful shaking. This shadow of the valley.

ONLY AND AGAIN

iii.

The Kings & Princes shall dress alike,
Des Roys & Princes dresseront simulacres,
Diviners, hollowing out, lifting the intestines;
Augures, creuez, esleuez aruspices;
Of a horned beast of gold & blue shining,
Corne victime d'oree & d'azur d'acre,
They shall interpret the entrails.
Interpretez seront les extipices.

Nostradamus Quatrain #3-26

ONLY AND AGAIN

But the prince you are in sweet regalia,
in bloom I canter to your flower,
heart of sagacity, thought of my being,
the world is not the claims it makes against you.

But do I speak? o the silence is venom between us.
I fall poised for the shape of your cross,
holding between us a stem from the immaculate flower
coaxed with dew and weighted with gold.

Light passes between our eyes: salvation is only promise.
Your face is a stairwell to the most perplexing possibility.
What do I know that I do not understand?

Your skirt captures my shadows in folds.
Dreams are the ocean, spit of the sea,
everything holding is holding me.

ONLY AND AGAIN

She is your rival, prince.
May God send you a better companion!
The lives of fruitful imagination
will carry the night like stardust on your brow.

You keep her in a cage like a bird—
thoughtless beaks chatter in oceanic splendor,
surrounded by the goats of tomorrow.

You won't cry the river of blood tonight, o sister,
your eyes are in tourniquets:
mastering majesty, storms of halo.

Cry but don't seem jaded. Flight will come soon.
He will return to your life as a moon
in the eclipse
as you nod your head to sleep.

ONLY AND AGAIN

The twins are virgins, together facing the west.
They are dressed like golden oxen—
shedding thought after thought in the heat
like sweat from her breasts.
Who is your dream child? Do you please mothers
in their fancies? I don't invite tears...or do I?

Your milk is my harbor: eyes rest gently on your hair,
thinking this is the moment where chrysanthemums float
from the sky to the ends of the earth.

Your niceties are pleasant to the torn spider,
from webs appertaining to delight:
she will slowly and languidly pass
in the stolen air like a kite.
o but violence is not the means to an end.

If God is a spider-woman, she undresses me
like a tall tale, disrobing and dismantling my perfumed body
from the silken hours. She is a complex being, androgynous
and free. God unravels her webs in thin salvation.
Do I know her face? What is it I fear?

Arachnophobia is the shuddering of my eyes
as I see her in the hells of this room—
hiding, thinking, blissfully waiting for prey.

ONLY AND AGAIN

Her waist is where I plant my torch.
I seek the oblivion of boasting
but no braggart can catch your magick.
The times are contained within the withering earth
like a skim satiation. Houses are imperiled by free will.

Contradiction is something we do not understand.
You tell us to watch television—
night is becoming you, you are dying, the rose
is between your lips:
we will tango.

Children know as they only recently left the room.
They fill the world with wonders of joy,
and we know their stupendous flight
like witches from the sky—
and they seek the most innocent alarms.

Don't look twice to the same river.
It is gone.

ONLY AND AGAIN

I hold my tongue. It is fruitful for painting
the questions of my heart.
You sing to me in the weary dark—
we can't kiss because the sensation is too deep.

o Woman of windswept eyes,
your longing is one with me.
We won't touch, distance sweet,
as I trust the entrails of this sacredness.

You grab me by the intestines,
thrust your knife into my gut
and make me what was once a slave
and would always be.

War isn't truth to this sad escapade
but the skies are in denial of dear dross
left by legs of our God.
o trickster, your mastery of time is unknown
but rediscovered.

ONLY AND AGAIN

And the world plays with time,
weary of the platitudes of political dance.
Everything is about the state of things,
the State.
But what is this power of your intense touch?
How do you gear your mantle
with boldness? Are the minds you entice
something beyond you or are you one with time?

I stand at the steps of your heart, love stroking my fingers.
Telling me the stopgap is nothing.
Don't open your eyes. Sleep. Feed the beast within, the beast
withering.

Face the sounds of drudgery.
Your eyes collapse into particles
from the wave of your lips.
Destiny is fruitful.

ONLY AND AGAIN

angels...
they don't exist in the eyes.
they hide behind your lashes...
how were you born?
<did mother kiss you quiet
                did father leave you standing, unalone?...>
I am greater than the sum of my parts.

Your windswept frenzy.
The medicine you hold in the palm.
I address you quickly as if there is nothing to lose.
How did you come into my world?

By sunlight, dear fairy, like a queen of spring.

The magick realm is one of hypnosis—
yet your queer ways make madness into a thriving world.

How do I count your sorrows with my lips?
By these words I swear to love you for the dawn will never know.

ONLY AND AGAIN

Quiet are the ancients.
Long for solitude, drinking the night into a cape
of horror.
Do you abuse your power, Mab of my heart?
How do you stand in the flesh to witness this intensity!

Darkness encloses your skin like a sea:
thickening in the former quietude
where your innocence was lost.
I am struggling to dismiss your glance.

Your power antagonizes me.
I am a worthless peon—deep thrush
of hush in the mad, mad emptiness.

I cage you to the splendor of seasons.
I am capturing the light of your heart.

ONLY AND AGAIN

Further into the dark.
The ambassador of my flesh
carries haste.
I do not wait for my virgin temperament
to lose itself to your fate.
Father of war, war as father,
the destiny of truth is to seek.
I am on the precipice of your livid way.

...but you do not know the winter.

Are you afraid of the answer you will receive
if you propose to the sun?

I write a book to your memory
so they will know your beauty
and sad song.

ONLY AND AGAIN

Grace abounds where sin places his hand.
Your hand is my mothering.
Touch my glory, and seek the light
like a sickness.
Carry the grief of your heart
into bliss. A classic trust in the argument.

I am not laughing at the point you made.
Your eyes are stolen from stars and emeralds.
Are you an envious worm? Does your flesh seek finality?
Have too many deaths caused an embarrassing fear?

Listen to the gorgons as they gouge out the eyes
of fear. Mother, you are temperamental in truth.
Veracity is not the strongman of wisdom.
Something in this wicked garden seduces me full.

ONLY AND AGAIN

iv. Carmel Lips

The languishing blank sophistry of your smile.
Snail's lip service to your hours as you hand me an abacus.
They trip the times into woeful worry.
The night is a sad mischief on the horizon,
culminating in gloom and eyes.

Her niceties are undone.
Her eyes are the treasures of bliss.
Do you kiss me when I bow to the edge?
I canter to the unknown.
Horror, horror and a smile, grim to the gladness.
Trim your ancient echelon.

She climbs the stairway to hearts unheard.
The misfits make us what we are.
Do you see the hourglass of her hips?
What does time tell you as it runs cold?
She grows old, dreams of purple envy.

The Gregorian calendar creeps slowly by.
On and on, the horses travel to the inn
where alleyways were unknown.
The forces of pleasure capture her serene antagonism.

o but know the clouds for their pass.

ONLY AND AGAIN

If only I could kiss you, Dawn, you are a vision.
The man of my sorrows brightens against the solace.
Do I feel the emptiness against my skin?
(Tell me like a gun you feel me deep within you.)

I sip the dusk like stolen eyes
from the cup of desolation.
His garden is reserved for weeping.
A dream was all this was,
and I miss your clouded time.

Carmel lips kiss my sleep.
Her sanctimonious kleptomania is lucid to the gray.
An eagle to the distress of my forefather,
kiss me again you ancient platitude.
Only boredom knows.

Ennui of the eyes, this terror.
You don't steal anymore, my carnal satisfaction.
Do we know the pleasure of fear?

Only if I catch you in the window looking for glory.

ONLY AND AGAIN

"Elements! your wrath suspend!"
Percy Bhysshe Shelley, "Queen Mab"

Density crosses the wire and a thousand sighs
capture out lust, catapulting it across the oaky floors.

We talk to one another in this ancient of ways.

If I carry my firs to your body,
wrapped around in thin perfume,
your neck a hypotenuse of glory,
I kiss, I kiss, you leave.

I don't know the sentiment from real terror.
I recollect the dream—
it comes slowly, like a passing train.

<ancient. cold dusky midnight. the stars are unseen.
your deepness is something sharp and terrible.
a dozen roses curtain across your hips.>

I am greater than the burden I carry.
However, your eyes are kites asking the wind for mercy.
We steal your pleasure, o woman of one thousand flights—
your entanglements are past me.

I don't know your fury.

ONLY AND AGAIN

An archetype of pleasure surmounts your eyes,
lingering in the vacancy of homes.
I am empty of you. You do not exist like eiderdown.

My hiddenness lay deep within you.
If only for a moment your coldness is deep.
I don't look for tomorrow if it will not come.

Everyone is asking about our hiatus.
They are like Egyptians carrying water.
The sand is time reigning the laws lewdly.

Don't touch the stars with the palm of your hand.
Your fist can work wonders.
However, you will not think deeply on things without root.
If anyone exists we excavate time.

I am a role you play—puppeteer,
do you twist my arms like springtime fever?
Ultimatums issued teach the worrisome.
I look both ways before crossing myself.

ONLY AND AGAIN

Her errors are more splendid than her ways.
I do not ask for more.
Spiders knit the fascination of her kindness.
Wrath is a purple lion of one thousand days.
Fathers reach to the mind of pithy.

Do your trumpeting for the end of days.
I will not ask for more than a sorrow's penny.

Your eyes dart one way, fascinate.
I have qualms with the rivers of dusk
following you to tarry the broken wrist.
My agony is something evil envies secretly
while severing the world from its space.

Privacy is not ours to keep.
In deep pastures we long to weep.

ONLY AND AGAIN

This moment is final. I aggrieve your sorrow.
I will fight to the death to winter your grin.
We grow old together and the magic steeps into cold.
Husks of violence, the crimes of salvation.

We don't know what mentor keeps us in gray.
I hold the glass of wine like a man of wealth.
Demand I kiss your eyes, closed they will be.
I don't understand your most frightening ladder.
I climb the haste of day.

I don't know what your sorrow brings.
It brings me sorrow as you are my sparrow, my bridge.
Do they ask of you for communion?
But do I foment the weeping of her shadow?

Chrysanthemums fill the sky with haze.

Addendum:

A white chrysanthemum is a symbol of loyalty and devoted love.

COUCHED LIKE ROBINSON CRUSOE

for Monica Lewis

i. Pastures of Plenty

"For sudden Joys, like Griefs, confound at first."
Daniel Defoe, *Robinson Crusoe*

"All evils are to be considered with the good that is in them, and with what worse attends them."
Daniel Defoe, *Robinson Crusoe*

"Generosity is giving more than you can, and pride is taking less than you need."
Khalil Gibran

ONLY AND AGAIN

I always resist the truth. Of fear.
Confound the world that bore-me,
the salt lick wounds of my passion.
I raised the death of skull.
I am not a secret—that is something only the mice carry.
Your face, an easy presence,
some light, mother, empty sea of longing.
I don't love to love—the magic is what it will be.
You hold me in some vacant eye
like a sharp knife gleamed with Icaruslight
from the pastures of fear.
Don't fall from the scathing surrender I become.
Your eyes don't make enemies of my drowning.

You already know I am here. Loneliness is an island.
I am talking to myself while you puncture my fruits.
I picked them, rotting, from the tree of magnitude.
Higher is the ghost. Grenade me to sleep.
Think outside of the box. Think, think, think.
And when you wake, forgive me for I am no longer with you.

ONLY AND AGAIN

I gave you my heart, beating, it was love,
and like the Louvre it is a raptless sequesturation of sense.
I can't have you and I know this.
Because eagles are forever.
And you are a clock of aggravation.
I won't hold you.
The magic is a funeral of secrecy.
I can't keep this behind me like a loaded gyun.

If madness is love, love is madness,
don't listen to the cherry trees blossom.
Instead, sing to yourself a long song
of forbidden forests. Where I hide.
Your aching for me is simple.
I can't remember you without a certain fondness of touch.

And oh, the splendoe of your insolent figure:
pressed like coupons to the room of night:
I don't curry favor with the spirits:
they don't holdme in flight:
I am wicked to their wings
and I only fly when I am darkness.

Singe me sweet earth
and scorch the promise of tomorrow.
I dedicate my wreath of roses to you.
Again, if angels were bodies of dream
only you can signal my solace
from the balcony of price.

ONLY AND AGAIN

If only resistance.
But no, I only turn and turn.
My fear. It is not the pearls of pleasure.
At dawn I steal your eyes
from the market of my honesty.

Catch me in the pillows of creature.
I tame the wet sanity of terror with your figment.
You purr to my temper. We are resurrect.
The stairway to the culprit of madness.
Something in the archway of fantasy.

If you stretch, I will catch a glimpse of your perfect voice.
I hear your madness in the calm breeze.
Don't fight with my artifice.
The silences are envious of our secrets.
Pandora does not keep watch over our mercy.
Oblivion rests like a tomcat on the highway.
A face is only love when it strikes the moon
with fanciful distress. Don't kiss me goodnight.
Storms play fugues over your lips.

ONLY AND AGAIN

What am I when the minor chords
of destiny race to beat the imaginary drum?
If you are sad, I am blue.
My blood races in the house of fear.
Torment rages in these blessings:
ambiguity is a desert,
I search for emptiness:
don't, just don't.
Don't fly from my eyes.

You are in tears, raptured by my playfulness.
I don't want to feel this way.
It isn't a dream I seek. It isn't love making me hang
from the windswept angel of fashion.
I don't listen to the chaos of wounds.

Circle my carapace with dolor and demand.
I won't fault you for leaving me.
If I give you my life, you will take it.
I don't know love, it is a fossil of my fear.

Blue. It is witness to your perfume.
Imagine knowing you are a gaze of starlight.
Would a feeling of unity encompass you? What is ice?
The missives of counterforce. Resistance.
I am in love and it is no other to me
than this childish game of tears.

ONLY AND AGAIN

ONLY AND AGAIN

I'll race you to the endtimes.
God closes the curtain and makes the final
castcall. A cat pounces your babyeyes
and a crystal is embedded in the chess game of pleasure.
The word is my choice. Don't sigh heavy. Beads of sweat.

The passage of greatness is a silence.
I don't sleep with the lights hidden over me.
I don't worship empty noise
and I steer the clouds like a magician.
Stop. Don't be quiet.

Keep talking. Don't let me down here.
My anxiety is suffocating. Your heart is pacing my vision.
I sense you, dark, in the craters of my yearning. Tomorrow, be wise.

The ferris wheels of your hibernation
are stolen from my eyes,
and I whisper the tumescence of travel
to your birded ways.

I build. The ship is not my path.
Pearls are lips of sea—worshiping the caverns, again,
I don't sense the pagan rite.
I lost you—you are the Ru Paul of destiny.
Don't become what you have been.
What has already to be is lost by lot—and it is time to sleep.

Dustin Pickering

ONLY AND AGAIN

If only. I feel nauseous. The rain keeps me awake.
Child of my eyes, don't cry the tears of memory.
Zeus was born of failure. Your own greatness.
Suicide is my guardian. Present me with the makeshift lie.
I don't want to gain the last rite.
Ritual is the contest of our laughter,
feeling the corners of day. Time is a last echo in the mountains.

If you catch the night in its sorcery:
don't ask it to condemn my lies.
I told myself you weren't the lizard of makeup.
These tunes are voices of eagerness.
I don't listen. Fabricate a majestic queen of surprise.
But no, the flash of the horizon is only a knowledge of forgetting.
You aren't the ghost of my imagination.
What did you promise? A magic box of ears
to listen to my bleating as I fell in love with you?

But what is this love? A virgin of milk and honey?
Do I know the rapture that constitutes forgiveness?
Whose religion will forgive me for loving you?
I steer into sleep, almost in memory, but I don't recall your glance.
The crystal palace is an empty sluice.

ONLY AND AGAIN

what befalls, night? the glance.
whatever is in darkness hides, circumstance,
we are all the icons of enemies.
symbols of destitution.
empty faces. horses of energy. fathomless sycophants.
my crux is your star. I hold you with bright delirium.
nothing is greater than mastery,
and I do not see.
yet what isn't bringing the money to the free
isn't what we need to know—part enchantment.
the night is a still wanderer. waiting for dewath.

his crusade is a magic flight. like flint, he is a rock.

the belief in supernovas, a worship of wood.
the smell of enigma is one highway from bliss.
if I don't understand you, I am within the flesh.
hold the emptiness of death. before you.
my eager eyes don't seek admissions.
but you are a love story to my decadence.
each thing is a paradox of doctors.
refine my angels of arching splendor.
the neck is tied to the bottom of apparel.
cold. raindrops are starving from finishing.

ONLY AND AGAIN

a ship is falling from the clouds.
emptiness abounds. nothing is in the closet.
a face is gleaming the patterns.
I am nothingness, a selfishness. broken.
my enigma is gold. artifice of shoulders,
beaming as a soft cry.
the told tales of terror. my ears and eyes.

I shrug away the fishes. don't know the circle.
race me to the beginning of time. flashes of passion.
the single warrior. all totalities are frozen.
don't ask what is being said. you won't whisper.
the whip is a farce of the fallen.
don't speak to the dead. they are silent. primrose.
a curtain of enthusiasm. jacks and jills.
cigarettes of purpose and plum. the edge of days.

I don't listen to the radios of rock. frozen barriers.
seas of slippery slopes. nighttime. please shadows.
gogol worshipped the golden gait. his promise.

if everything doesn't gleam.
but you know the drill. no one is apathy.
we all catch kites of fascism. no. the evil.
do not address the morals. mirror of perfection.
your imagination is at last lost.
don't speak to the knights of song.

ONLY AND AGAIN

don't worry she will know me.
the cat's meow. pissy angelface. don't tease the wind.
your house is yom kipper war. Donald dreamer.
the magician of plastic. make the soul bend into a house.
you will know the evil of triumph. greed is perchance.
the victim is war.
but only I know the sounds of the fallen. enemies. what is the day?
a sunshine of your membranes?
black days of comfort. nothing is a shadow.
who is the rose of your passion? a room of deep.

if I was a blight on the stairwell. I don't perhaps.
there is no "perhaps" only a tomorrow of definite.
stolen fragile time. a clock of rapture.
the doors are not the maker's.
if I dream I am not sleeping. waken me with shadows.
the sex of gorgeous playfulness. these dice of flash.
I don't gamble the perfect. prefect of torment.
your quiet rose of stem the dream.

if beauty were a thing of grace. but good is tasteless.
I sip the lips of your eclipse. nothing rots.
a perfect apathy. time is a foreshadowing of fatherlands.
you don't know the race to rack. the silence. killer. mad.

a blossom plunders the door of food. follow. folly is loud.
you won't vacate the ocean of my sorrow.
if hypnosis steals the oval flippancy, resurrect.
there is no flippancy toward resurrection.
I laugh at your death. perfect wombs. trust the thieves.
shadowland is a box of tides. sea is the song.

if you see the sealing of peace, don't whisper to the wound.
instead, lean toward the flustered eyelid.

Dustin Pickering

ONLY AND AGAIN

you aren't everyday. instead the bliss is iconic.
wind a dream in the fortress. fastidious. nothing is dense.
stars enter the galactic glass of my terror. empty again.
your perfection is my own psychic fashion.
don't enter the last exit of softness.
ignore my bliss. don't triumph at the archway.

if the restaurants of all being suffice. you don't demand.
kite. the merging of day and yinyang happiness.
I can't fart the favorites. a song of deep.
the warrior in me is a sleep. I don't game these gods.
they are intuitive as a blister.
trust lecture on madness. these fractals are sighs of opera.

music of deep. jack and jills. the angel of penury.
pensive doubts—these are knights of treasury.
if only a highway was the sound of dementia.
tokens of prematurity.
writing is transgressing against time. worry for an afterlife.

ONLY AND AGAIN

passion is a night time fire escape.
empty thoughts conjure mad idiocy.
laughter outside of the box—what tries?
if angel. the battalions of promise.
intuition lies like a great snake. withdraw your prince.
democracy is a snail on the magi's silence.
their box of pestilence offers fissures.
a night is stolen in the collapse. structures untie.
a beacon of faces. everyone is a snake.
light tempts the pastures of plenty. golden,
the bloke of posturing.
your eyes focused like a cat's.

donne was a sigh of grief. jobs are arising after corridors.
if only the slight of fancy was your furtive glare.
but you know nothing of the horrors we share.
anarchism of favors. this is what we do again.
if you are restless the merciful fathers will know.
everyone is quiet in the solace. winter.
don't steal the show. if you are couched in idiom,
the precious diamonds are the ways of men.
all eager to the continuum. afterlife seizure.
if the sand steals your sorrow, scream.
existential delusion isn't feared by many.

loss is a high court. but only the mirror knows.
you lack a fundament of pleasure. rudiments of god.
the innocents were suffering. loss is final. no touching the gate.
if you eat the fizzle furor my brain will swallow.
all tomorrow is a toddler, again is shy.

heaven is a blissful paradigm. roses a'bloom in the courtyard.
you aren't the sufferer of this ocean. all nighter. signals,
the escapades of doom.
if engines are roaring, the imagination is a decade old.
fiery combustion of fossil. nothing is a dream. only.

italics of this mess, I don't hate the shiny thing.
don't ask for money or faith. share your gold teeth.
smile like a reindeer. the happiness of third degrees.
your vendors empty their own medicine cabinets.

inspiration

inspiration feels like a
        forever machine
but it's a relentless echo
in canyons of despondent dream

flowers of forlornness
        i press my lips
          to silence

an aggrieved nothingness
in the placid dark

inspiration strikes the mercury
hot and earthy—
        grim to the dawn witch.

a cold faceless thought
        my overt casualty
        brains breaking spleen

the lifting of darkness
        against cemetery sound

crowing and combing
        the nastiness of ground

being is what defines
        nothingness

apex of time

night after night
loneliness takes winter hostage

i am nothing
a sack of dirt aching for tomorrow

the membranes of bewilderment
stir in fancy chariots

        thinking of silver radiance

gray as the golden forever forest
filled with turgid gloom

the light self-destructs
burning flowers, again a rising tide

if water can cure the temperament
a flesh flitting alone in golden
        mountains—
                meadows rising
                all things considered

you were dead but earth knew you
and birthed you

and desire was an empty gullet
pride silenced at the apex of time

gestalt

the gestalt bearing
silver minded
      again an old thought
      circumvents the dream

i cry in your rain
seeking tears

you know my heart echoed
your fine words
      a suicide against stone

ripples of solace through memory
grief complete fathomless
      stars slouch as roses torch
      tomorrows

peering westward
      thinking of pride

i can't forget your last heirloom
haunted nirvana of your kiss
      but you are shadows

      the fear freezes me
      like a tree whimpering

broken stone

i can't think of you
right now
        because
                thoughts are all i have

and forever, forever, forever

your heart is forecast of my being
you, a slight tomorrow,
                something doomed by god

if everyone forgets
we are all forgotten
                so whose memory remains?

stillness is naught but an eye
for madness

i felt you in my tremor
your daughter slept against my fear

i cannot suffer to know this ancient wisdom—
this broken stone of days gone by

EPILOGUE
The Kristal Palace

Only I had eyes to see. There were only a few invitations sent out, and some of us didn't show up. There was a tall box with a small clock on top. Inside that box were books that held unforgivable secrets. We weren't allowed to read them. We were instructed to sit at the table and be still. We were permitted to talk amongst ourselves and get to know each other but none of us knew why we were there or what purpose our presence served. It was a quiet nihilism we felt and shared.

Eventually Hitler spoke. He shook his head and declared that all the arts were dead. I asked who killed them. He couldn't answer. Emily Dickinson shrugged her shoulder and suddenly exclaimed, "They've always been dead. Ambassadors of culture were never cool."

Sylvia Plath and Emily Dickinson got along really well. Emily liked to sew and talk about her mortal love affair. Sylvia chimed in with her story about breaking her leg and visiting cadavers with her boyfriend. Emily suddenly stopped talking. Sylvia appeared confused. She said, "Is it something I said, dear?" Emily said she was always jealous of Sylvia because of her red hair. She said it was like Ophelia's, who Emily often daydreamed about. She said drowning was a peaceful way to die and she wished she had tried it. Sylvia brought up Virginia Woolf. Emily asked who was afraid of Virginia to the collective laughter of the entire circle.

Suddenly Thoreau stood up and delivered an impromptu sermon.

"This symposium, granted, is lacking character. We don't know who called for it. We don't know it's purpose. I vote we take control of it. It is our destiny to deliver our own fates."

Emily nodded in silence. Hitler shrugged. He said, "No, the fate belongs to the greatest man. We are yet to see who he is."

Sylvia laughed hysterically. "Man? Who said man was the greatest?" Emily nodded.

Hitler sat back down quietly. He plucked at his moustache. "This is pointless. I couldn't begin to tell you that arguing is a waste of energy in our case," he said. Then he smoothed a crease in his shirt.

Good and evil don't know each other very well, sometimes.

Thoreau suddenly shouted, "We are in the Kristal Palace! This is where the world ends."

An alarm suddenly struck and we were silent again. I tugged at my hat and belt. Sylvia turned to me and asked in a whisper, "Why do men think so much of themselves?" I politely answered that we had nothing else to think of, not understanding the question as men do.

Every time I tried to speak, I was interrupted by one of the crowd. Emily finally laughed loudly when she recognized I had something to say.

"Who are we waiting for?"

"Who says we are waiting for anyone? Sometimes life is a pointless masquerade," Sylvia cooed. Then she lowered her eyes to the ground. Emily waved her arms around.

"It's always something, right? First it's a dream, then the speed of light, then some kind of magical holograph. What is life?" She sat back down and scratched at her thickly plaited dress. "I could've been a man, you know?" She exclaimed.

"No one doubts you Emily. I'm more concerned about the quiet one, the one they called the Lone Wolf." I didn't speak. "Who is he? Whose head are we in?"

Hitler stood up impatiently. He noticed there were wine glasses on the table. He carefully picked one up and examined it. "I could make a statement," he said. "By smashing this glass, I am expressing a fundamental discontent with my condition."

Sylvia chuckled. "That's called existentialism."

"Whatever it is called, I'm not having any part of it!" Thoreau exclaimed. "It's unfortunate that I can't stand any of you but I am required to wait with you. This is an injustice and no small one at that."

"Shutup, Henry. Act like a human. This isn't the time and place for senseless protest," Hitler retorted. He lifted the glass to his eye level. "Shame, it is such a beautiful glass."

"Beauty is a thing of chance and short life," Emily said and returned to her prayerful repose.

"Oh no, this isn't beauty. It's strength. It's valor. It's a vision of war," Hitler responded eagerly. "I could use this transparent god to awaken the doubts of humankind." Hitler took a deep breath.

"But, you forget something. We were told not to bother the silverware." Emily turned to Hitler as she spoke. "If you break that, we are all doomed."

Hitler quietly sat back down. "Who invented these rules?" He asked with a quizzical stare. Suddenly everyone turned and looked at the empty box against the wall. The clock ticked slowly. Everyone was dead silent as it clicked.

"By Silenus, I call this a ruse!" Thoreau stood up, pointed to the clock, measured calculations in his eye. "A ruse. What do you others say?"

"Love will abide us in patience," Sylvia said sullenly. Emily scoffed.

"Love, a cheap nothing. Love dies with the birds. Sunlight only is eternal."

"Emily, always a cynic. Always scoffing at life," Hitler said. "I could break this glass and everything would cease. Our waiting would end."

"We don't want the waiting to end." Sylvia shifted her body. "Only *you* want a decadent ending to this cosmic affair. Who are we anyway? What is identity to us? Are we one and the same? Who keeps our names?"

A bell chimed for the third time. Thoreau shouted, "Third time's the charm! This is the end of our peril at last."

Suddenly, Jim Morrison who had gone unnoticed throughout the conversation, spoke with calm resolution. "This is the end. Beauty, rage, perfection. Love is a striking of the clock. Now we open the box and see what the mystery of this meeting is all about. Who will do the honors?"

Hitler rose in rage. "You—decadent musician! You brought us here without our permission. You conjured us, you alone. Why do you want us here?"

"It was not me who brought us together. Just because I know the rules of the game does not mean I invented it." Jim gave Hitler a shadowy eye. "If you break the glass, we will never know the mystery."

ONLY AND AGAIN

Hitler's eyes filled with an angsty storm that frightened everyone at the table. Thoreau said, "Look, we've already been here, Adolf! We know what you are going to do. This happens every time. Do you learn? No. And we have to come back, again and again. You have choices."

Nietzsche entered the room. Jim's eyes lit up in excitement. "Friedrich! The gang's all here. We know what is about to happen."

Nietzsche ran his finger across his throat. Hitler, eyes gleaming with hate and rage, picked up the crystal glass. Suddenly Emily shrieked loudly. Sylvia covered her ears.

Hitler tossed the glass to the ground in sullen resolution. It shattered into dozens of pieces. Jim, staring with the eyes of a lizard, shook his head knowingly. "It's always you," he said.

Jim reached for the clock that ticked endlessly on the top of the box. He grabbed its winder on the back. He clinched it hard until it stopped moving. The world turned black.

ONLY I HAD EYES TO SEE...

ONLY AND AGAIN

www.ingramcontent.com/pod-product-compliance
Lightning Source LLC
LaVergne TN
LVHW020937090426
835512LV00020B/3393